THE BATSFORD BOOK OF
Religious Verse

Head of Christ. *Piero della Francesca*

The Batsford Book of
Religious Verse

Edited by Elizabeth Jennings

B.T. BATSFORD LTD, LONDON

First published 1981
Selection © Elizabeth Jennings 1981
ISBN 0 7134 3889 4

Filmset in Monophoto Sabon, 11 on 12pt, by
Servis Filmsetting Ltd, Manchester
Printed in Great Britain by
Butler & Tanner Ltd, Frome, Somerset
for the publishers B.T. Batsford Ltd
4 Fitzhardinge Street, London W1H 0AH

Contents

The Illustrations

The endpapers are reproduced from panels on the predella of an altar-piece by Fra Angelico (1387–1455). *The National Gallery, London*

Introduction

Religious poetry or, as I prefer to call it, poems on religious themes, must always be judged by the same critical criteria which we bring to bear on poems concerned with any other subject. We must, without too much strain, make 'a willing suspension of disbelief'. One does not have to be in love to watch or read *Romeo and Juliet* or Chaucer's *Troilus and Creysede*, one need not have visited Rome to enjoy Browning's *Two in the Campagna*, but it does of course help if one *has* been in love or visited Italy.

The poems assembled here are drawn from almost every period of British literature. They are mostly lyrical ones, part of that great, unbroken tradition of such verse that runs like a seam of gold through all other movements, literary battles, critical attacks. This British tradition cannot be stopped or damaged. An atheist must be able to enjoy a sonnet by Hopkins or a piece of *vers libre* by Eliot. The poems I am concerned with are not devotional poems, substitutes for prayer. They do not teach, they do not seek to convert. They are records of the spiritual experience of a poet who has great talent and in some cases, undoubted genius.

I have, however, included poems by Matthew Arnold although they are the work of an agnostic. In the Victorian age, religious doubt had something of the pain and passion of a religion. Doubt was a vital part of the nineteenth-century's mood, tempo, and experience. In fact, Arnold's *Dover Beach* is a great poem, a tragic cry which has the poignancy of apparently unanswered prayer.

The richest source of English religious verse is undoubtedly the seventeenth century, and it has been particularly hard to do justice to that period without giving it too great a representation.

With the twentieth century, it is, sometimes, difficult to find true religious verse because this age is not an age of faith; it is a period of fear, anxiety, materialism, and, in tangible and material matters, an age of enlightenment. Science has brought great good in medical matters, but great terror in nuclear fission. The voices of religious poets are therefore, voices of people 'crying in the wilderness'. Nonetheless they have, particularly in the case of Eliot, cast some radiance over areas of doubt, unbelief and fear.

The poems in this anthology are arranged chronologically, in that Old Testament subjects are placed before New Testament

The Nativity. *Louis Le Nain*

ones. Others, which are personal expressions of love, grief or penitence, or which depict some sort of mystical experience or encounter with God, are placed where they seemed to reflect or fit the more easily categorised poems.

The aim of this book is to give pleasure, perhaps even excitement. What it does not attempt to do is to teach or to convert. Poetry, whatever its theme, offers experience, not sermons.

ELIZABETH JENNINGS

Man

My God, I heard this day,
That none doth build a stately habitation,
  But he that means to dwell therein.
  What house more stately hath there been,
Or can be, then is Man? to whose creation
  All things are in decay.

  For man is ev'ry thing,
And more: He is a tree, yet bears more fruit;
  A beast, yet is, or should be more:
  Reason and speech we onely bring.
Parrats may thank us, if they are not mute,
  They go upon the score.

  Man is all symmetrie,
Full of proportions, one limbe to another,
  And all to all the world besides:
  Each part may call the furthest, brother:
For head with foot hath private amitie,
  And both with moons and tides.

  Nothing hath got so farre,
But man hath caught and kept it, as his prey.
  His eyes dismount the highest starre:
  He is in little all the sphere.
Herbs gladly cure our flesh; because that they
  Finde their acquaintance there.

  For us the windes do blow,
The earth doth rest, heav'n move, and fountains flow.
  Nothing we see, but means our good,
  As our delight, or as our treasure:
The whole is, either our cupboard of food,
  Or cabinet of pleasure.

The starres have us to bed;
Night draws the curtain, which the sunne withdraws;
Musick and light attend our head.
All things unto our flesh are kinde
In their descent and being; to our minde
In their ascent and cause.

Each thing is full of dutie:
Waters united are our navigation;
Distinguished, our habitation;
Below, our drink; above, our meat;
Both are our cleanlinesse. Hath one such beautie?
Then how are all things neat?

More servants wait on Man,
Then he'l take notice of: in ev'ry path
He treads down that which doth befriend him,
When sicknesse makes him pale and wan.
Oh mightie love! Man is one world, and hath
Another to attend him.

Since then, my God, thou hast
So brave a Palace built; O dwell in it,
That it may dwell with thee at last!
Till then, afford us so much wit;
That, as the world serves us, we may serve thee,
And both thy servants be.

GEORGE HERBERT (1593–1632)

Eve

I am Eve, great Adam's wife,
I that wrought my children's loss,
I that wronged Jesus of life,
Mine by right had been the cross.

I a kingly house forsook,
Ill my choice and my disgrace,
Ill the counsel that I took
Withering me and all my race . . .

I that brought winter in
And the windy glistening sky,
I that brought sorrow and sin,
Hell and pain and terror, I.

Version: THOMAS MacDONAGH (1878–1916)

Adam and Eve. *John Martin*

To God the Father

Great God, within whose simple essence we
Nothing but that which is thyself can find;
When on thyself thou didst reflect thy mind,
Thy thought was God, and took the form of thee:
And when this God, thus born, thou lov'st, and he
Loved thee again, with passion of like kind
(As lovers' sighs which meet become one wind),
Both breathed one sprite of equal deity.
Eternal Father, whence these two do come
And wilt the title of my father have,
And heavenly knowledge in my mind engrave,
That it thy son's true Image may become:
   And cense my heart with sighs of holy love,
   That it the temple of the Sprite may prove.

HENRY CONSTABLE (1562–1613)

Christ in Glory. *Liberale da Verona*

The Seven Virgins

All under the leaves, the leaves of life,
  I met with the virgins seven,
And one of them was Mary mild,
  Our Lord's mother from heaven.

O what are you seeking, you seven fair maids,
  All under the leaves of life?
Come tell, come tell me what seek you
  All under the leaves of life.

We're seeking for no leaves, Thomas,
  But for a friend of thine,
We're seeking for sweet Jesus Christ,
  To be our guide and thine.

Go you down, go you down to yonder town,
  And sit in the gallery,
And there you'll find sweet Jesus Christ
  Nailed to a big yew-tree.

So down they went to yonder town
  As fast as foot could fall,
And many a grievous bitter tear
  From the virgins' eyes did fall.

O peace, mother, O peace, mother,
  Your weeping doth me grieve.
O I must suffer this, he said,
  For Adam and for Eve.

O how can I my weeping leave
  Or my sorrows undergo
Whilst I do see my own son die,
  When sons I have no mo'?

Dear mother, dear mother, you must take John,
  All for to be your son,
And he will comfort you sometimes,
  Mother, as I have done.

O come, thou John Evangelist,
  Thou'rt welcome unto me,
But more welcome my own dear son
  That I nursed upon my knee.

Then he laid his head on his right shoulder,
  Seeing death it struck him nigh:
The Holy Ghost be with your soul,
  I die, mother dear, I die.

Oh the rose, the rose, the gentle rose,
  And the fennel that grows so green,
God give us grace in every place
  To pray for our king and queen.

Furthermore for our enemies all
  Our prayers they should be strong.
Amen, Good Lord. Your charity
  Is the ending of my song.

ANONYMOUS

A Song for St Cecilia's Day, 1687

From harmony, from heav'nly harmony
    This universal frame began:
    When Nature underneath a heap
      Of jarring atoms lay,
    And could not heave her head,
The tuneful voice was heard from high:
    'Arise, ye more than dead.'
Then cold, and hot, and moist, and dry,

In order to their stations leap,
    And Music's pow'r obey.
From harmony, from heav'nly harmony
    This universal frame began:
    From harmony to harmony
Thro' all the compass of the notes it ran,
The diapason closing full in Man.

What passion cannot Music raise and quell!
    When Jubal struck the corded shell,
    His list'ning brethren stood around,
    And, wond'ring, on their faces fell
    To worship that celestial sound.
Less than a god they thought there could not dwell
    Within the hollow of that shell
    That spoke so sweetly and so well.
What passion cannot Music raise and quell!

    The Trumpet's loud clangour
      Excites us to arms,
    With shrill notes of anger,
      And mortal alarms.
    The double double double beat
      Of the thund'ring Drum
Cries: 'Hark! the foes come;
Charge, charge, 't is too late to retreat.'

Stained glass in Amington Church, Warwickshire. *William Morris*

The soft complaining Flute
In dying notes discovers
The woes of hopeless lovers,
Whose dirge is whisper'd by the warbling Lute.

Sharp Violins proclaim
Their jealous pangs, and desperation,
Fury, frantic indignation,
Depth of pains, and height of passion,
For the fair, disdainful dame.

But O! what art can teach,
What human voice can reach,
The sacred Organ's praise?
Notes inspiring holy love,
Notes that wing their heav'nly ways
To mend the choirs above.

Orpheus could lead the savage race;
And trees uprooted left their place,
Sequacious of the lyre;
But bright Cecilia rais'd the wonder high'r:
When to her Organ vocal breath was giv'n,
An angel heard, and straight appear'd,
Mistaking earth for heav'n.

Grand Chorus
As from the pow'r of sacred lays
The spheres began to move,
And sung the great Creator's praise
To all the blest above;
So, when the last and dreadful hour
This crumbling pageant shall devour,
The Trumpet shall be heard on high,
The dead shall live, the living die,
And Music shall untune the sky.

JOHN DRYDEN (1631–1700)

Man

Weighing the steadfastness and state
Of some mean things which here below reside,
Where birds like watchful clocks the noiseless date
   And intercourse of times divide,
Where bees at night get home and hive, and flowers
     Early, as well as late,
Rise with the sun, and set in the same bowers;

I would (said I) my God would give
The staidness of these things to man! for these
To his divine appointments ever cleave,
   And no new business breaks their peace;
The birds nor sow, nor reap, yet sup and dine,
     The flowers without clothes live,
Yet *Solomon* was never dressed so fine.

Man hath still either toys, or care,
He hath no root, nor to one place is tied,
But ever restless and irregular
   About this earth doth run and ride,
He knows he hath a home, but scarce knows where,
     He says it is so far
That he hath quite forgot how to go there.

He knocks at all doors, strays and roams,
Nay hath not so much wit as some stones have
Which in the darkest nights point to their homes,
   By some hid sense their Maker gave;
'Man is the shuttle, to whose winding quest
     And passage through these looms
God ordered motion, but ordained no rest.

HENRY VAUGHAN (1622–1695)

God the Father. *Illuminated MS.*

Sonnet

Batter my heart, three-person'd God; for, you
As yet but knock, breathe, shine, and seek to mend;
That I may rise, and stand, o'erthrow me, and bend
Your force, to break, blow, burn and make me new.
I, like an usurp'd town, to another due,
Labour to admit you, but Oh, to no end,
Reason your viceroy in me, me should defend,
But is captiv'd, and proves weak or untrue.
Yet dearly I love you, and would be loved fain,
But am betroth'd unto your enemy:
Divorce me, untie, or break that knot again,
Take me to you, imprison me, for I
Except you enthral me, never shall be free,
Nor ever chaste, except you ravish me.

JOHN DONNE (1573–1631)

The Divine Image

To Mercy, Pity, Peace, and Love
All pray in their distress;
And to these virtues of delight
Return their thankfulness.

For Mercy, Pity, Peace, and Love
Is God, our father dear,
And Mercy, Pity, Peace, and Love
Is Man, his child and care.

For Mercy has a human heart,
Pity a human face,
And Love, the human form divine,
And Peace, the human dress.

Then every man, of every clime,
That prays in his distress,
Prays to the human form divine,
Love, Mercy, Pity, Peace.

And all must love the human form,
In heathen, turk, or jew;
Where Mercy, Love, & Pity dwell
There God is dwelling too.

WILLIAM BLAKE (1757–1827)

Walking with God
Gen. v. 24

Oh! for a closer walk with God,
    A calm and heavenly frame;
A light to shine upon the road
    That leads me to the Lamb!

Where is the blessedness I knew
    When first I saw the Lord?
Where is the soul-refreshing view
    Of Jesus and his word?

What peaceful hours I once enjoyed!
    How sweet their memory still!
But they have left an aching void,
    The world can never fill.

Return, O holy Dove, return!
    Sweet messenger of rest:
I hate the sins that made thee mourn,
    And drove thee from my breast.

The dearest idol I have known,
    Whate'er that idol be,
Help me to tear it from thy throne,
    And worship only thee.

So shall my walk be close with God,
    Calm and serene my frame;
So purer light shall mark the road
    That leads me to the Lamb.

WILLIAM COWPER (1731–1800)

Holy Trinity, Sloane Street

MCMVII

An Acolyte singeth
Light six white tapers with the Flame of Art,
Send incense wreathing to the lily flowers,
And, with your cool hands white,
Swing the warm censer round my bruised heart,
Drop, dove-grey eyes, your penitential showers
On this pale acolyte.

A cofirmandus continueth
The tall red house soars upward to the stars,
The doors are chased with sardonyx and gold,
And in the long white room
Thin drapery draws backward to unfold
Cadogan Square between the window-bars
And Whistler's mother knitting in the gloom.

The Priest endeth
How many hearts turn Motherward to-day!
(Red roses faint not on your twining stems!)
Bronze triptych doors unswing!
Wait, restive heart, wait, rounded lips, to pray
Mid beaten copper interset with gems
Behold! Behold! your King!

JOHN BETJEMAN (1906–   )

Moonlight at Brighton. *John Constable*

It is a Beauteous Evening

It is a beauteous evening, calm and free,
The holy time is quiet as a Nun
Breathless with adoration; the broad sun
Is sinking down in its tranquillity;
The gentleness of heaven broods o'er the Sea:
Listen! the mighty Being is awake,
And doth with his eternal motion make
A sound like thunder – everlastingly.
Dear Child! dear Girl! that walkest with me here,
If thou appear untouched by solemn thought,
Thy nature is not therefore less divine:
Thou liest in Abraham's bosom all the year;
And worshipp'st at the Temple's inner shrine,
God being with thee when we know it not.

WILLIAM WORDSWORTH (1770–1850)

Psalm 130.
De Profundis Clamavi

From depth of sin and from a deep despair,
   From depth of death, from depth of heart's sorrow,
   From this deep cave of darkness' deep repair,
Thee have I called, O Lord, to be my borrow.
   Thou in my voice, O Lord, perceive and hear
   My heart, my hope, my plaint, my overthrow,
My will to rise, and let by grant appear
   That to my voice thine ears do well intend.
   No place so far that to thee is not near;
No depth so deep that thou ne mayst extend
   Thine ear thereto. Hear then my woeful plaint.
   For, Lord, if thou do observe what men offend
And put thy native mercy in restraint,
   If just exaction demand recompense,
   Who may endure, O Lord? Who shall not faint
At such account? Dread and not reverence
   Should so reign large. But thou seeks rather love
   For in thy hand is mercy's residence
By hope whereof thou dost our hearts move.
   I in thee, Lord, have set my confidence;
   My soul such trust doth evermore approve.
Thy holy word of eterne excellence,
   Thy mercy's promise that is always just,
   Have been my stay, my pillar, and pretence.
My soul in God hath more desirous trust
   Than hath the watchman looking for the day
   By the relief to quench of sleep the thrust.
Let Israel trust unto the Lord alway
   For grace and favour arn his property.
   Plenteous ransom shall come with him, I say,
And shall redeem all our iniquity.

SIR THOMAS WYATT (1503–1542)

Storm off Cromer. *J.S. Cotman*

To Marguerite, in returning a volume of the Letters of Ortis

Yes: in the sea of life enisl'd,
With echoing straits between us thrown,
Dotting the shoreless watery wild,
We mortal millions live *alone*.
 The islands feel the enclasping flow,
And then their endless bounds they know.

But when the moon their hollows lights
And they are swept by balms of spring,
And in their glens, on starry nights,
The nightingales divinely sing;
And lovely notes, from shore to shore,
Across the sounds and channels pour;

Oh then a longing like despair
Is to their farthest caverns sent;
For surely once, they feel, we were
Parts of a single continent.

Now round us spreads the watery plain –
Oh might our marges meet again!

Who order'd, that their longing's fire
Should be, as soon as kindled, cool'd?
Who renders vain their deep desire? –
　A God, a God their severance rul'd;
And bade betwixt their shores to be
The unplumb'd, salt, estranging sea.

MATTHEW ARNOLD (1822–1888)

God and the Devil

God and the Devil
Were talking one day
Ages and ages of years ago.
God said: Suppose
Things were fashioned this way,
Well then, so and so.
The Devil said: No,
Prove it if you can.
So God created Man
And that is how it all began.
It has continued now for many a year
And sometimes it seems more than we can bear.
But why should bowels yearn and cheeks grow pale?
We're here to point a moral and adorn a tale.

STEVIE SMITH (1903–1971)

The Forerunners

The harbingers are come. See, see their mark;
White is their colour, and behold my head.
But must they have my brain? must they dispark
Those sparkling notions, which therein were bred?
      Must dulnesse turn me to a clod?
Yet have they left me, *Thou art still my God.*

Good men ye be, to leave me my best room,
Ev'n all my heart, and what is lodged there:
I passe not, I, what of the rest become,
So Thou art still my God, be out of fear.
      He will be pleased with that dittie;
And if it please him, I write fine and wittie.

Farewell sweet phrases, lovely metaphors.
But will ye leave me thus? when ye before
Of stews and brothels onely knew the doores,
Then did I wash you with my tears, and more,
      Brought you to Church well drest and clad:
My God must have my best, ev'n all I had.

Lovely enchanting language, sugar-cane,
Hony of roses, whither wilt thou flie?
Hath some fond love tic'd thee to thy bane?
And wilt thou leave the Church, and love a stie?
      Fie, thou wilt soil thy broider'd coat.
And hurt thy self, and him that sings the note.

Let foolish lovers, if they will love dung,
With canvas, not with arras, clothe their shame:
Let follie speak in her own native tongue.
True beautie dwells on high: ours is a flame
      But borrow'd thence to light us thither.
Beautie and beauteous words should go together.

Yet if you go, I passe not; take your way:
For, *Thou art still my God*, is all that ye
Perhaps with more embellishment can say.
Go birds of spring: let winter have his fee;
      Let a bleak paleness chalk the doore,
So all within be livelier then before.

GEORGE HERBERT (1593–1633)

Unprofitableness

How rich, O Lord! how fresh thy visits are!
'Twas but just now my bleak leaves hopeless hung
      Sullied with dust and mud;
Each snarling blast shot through me, and did share
Their youth, and beauty, cold showers nipped, and wrung
      Their spiciness, and blood;
But since thou didst in one sweet glance survey
Their sad decays, I flourish, and once more
      Breathe all perfumes, and spice;
I smell a dew like *myrrh*, and all the day
Wear in my bosom a full Sun; such store
      Hath one beam from thy Eyes.
But, ah, my God! what fruit hast thou of this?
When one poor leaf did ever I yet fall
      To wait upon thy wreath?
Thus thou all day a thankless weed dost dress,
And when th' hast done, a stench, or fog is all
      The odour I bequeath.

HENRY VAUGHAN (1622–1695)

From: In Memoriam

I found Him not in world or sun,
  Or eagle's wing, or insect's eye;
  Nor thro' the questions men may try,
The petty cobwebs we have spun:

If e'er when faith had fall'n asleep,
  I heard a voice 'believe no more'
  And heard an ever-breaking shore
That tumbled in the Godless deep;

A warmth within the breast would melt
  The freezing reason's colder part,
  And like a man in wrath the heart
Stood up and answer'd 'I have felt.'

No, like a child in doubt and fear:
  But that blind clamour made me wise;
  Then was I as a child that cries,
But, crying, knows his father near;

And what I am beheld again
  What is, and no man understands;
  And out of darkness came the hands
That reach thro' nature, moulding men.

Love is and was my Lord and King,
  And in his presence I attend
  To hear the tidings of my friend,
Which every hour his couriers bring.

Love is and was my King and Lord,
  And will be, tho' as yet I keep
  Within his court on earth, and sleep
Encompass'd by his faithful guard,

And hear at times a sentinel
  Who moves about from place to place,
  And whispers to the world of space,
In the deep night, that all is well.

ALFRED, LORD TENNYSON (1809–1892)

from: Two Bookes of Ayres

View mee, Lord, a worke of thine;
Shall I then lye drown'd in night?
Might thy grace in mee but shine,
I should seeme made all of light.

But my soule still surfets so
On the poysoned baytes of sinne,
That I strange and ugly growe,
All in darke, and foule within.

Clense mee, Lord, that I may kneele
At thine Altar, pure and white:
They that once thy Mercies feele,
Gaze no more on earths delight.

Worldly joyes like shadowes fade,
When the heav'nly light appeares;
But the cov'nants thou hast made,
Endlesse, know nor dayes, nor yeares.

In thy word, Lord, is my trust,
To thy mercies fast I flye;
Though I am but clay and dust,
Yet thy grace can lift me high.

THOMAS CAMPION (1567–1620)

Orchard in Spring. *Mark Fisher*

Spring and Fall
to a young child

Márgarét, áre you gríeving
Over Goldengrove unleaving?
Leáves líke the things of man, you
With your fresh thoughts care for, can you?
Ah! ás the heart grows older
It will come to such sights colder
By and by, nor spare a sigh
Though worlds of wanwood leafmeal lie;
And yet you will weep and know why.
Now no matter, child, the name:
Sórrow's springs áre the same.
Nor mouth had, no nor mind, expressed
What heart heard of, ghost guessed:
It ís the blight man was born for,
It is Margaret you mourn for.

GERARD MANLEY HOPKINS (1844–1889)

The Annunciation

The angel and the girl are met.
Earth was the only meeting place.
For the embodied never yet
Travelled beyond the shore of space.
The eternal spirits in freedom go.

See, they have come together, see,
While the destroying minutes flow,
Each reflects the other's face
Till heaven in hers and earth in his
Shine steady there. He's come to her
From far beyond the farthest star,
Feathered through time. Immediacy
Of strangest strangeness is the bliss
That from their limbs all movement takes.
Yet the increasing rapture brings
So great a wonder that it makes
Each feather tremble on his wings.

Outside the window footsteps fall
Into the ordinary day
And with the sun along the wall
Pursue their unreturning way.
Sound's perpetual roundabout
Rolls its numberd octaves out
And hoarsely grinds its battered tune.

But through the endless afternoon
These neither speak nor movement make,
But stare into their deepening trance
As if their gaze would never break.

EDWIN MUIR (1887–1959)

from: Hamlet

Some say that ever 'gainst that season comes
Wherein our Savior's birth is celebrated,
The bird of dawning singeth all night long,
And then, they say, no spirit dare stir abroad,
The nights are wholesome, then no planets strike,
No fairy takes, nor witch hath power to charm:
So hallowed and so gracious is that time.

WILLIAM SHAKESPEARE (1564–1616)

Hill Christmas

They came over the snow to the bread's
purer snow, fumbled it in their huge
hands, put their lips to it
like beasts, stared into the dark chalice
where the wine shone, felt it sharp
on their tongue, shivered as at a sin
remembered, and heard love cry
momentarily in their hearts' manger.

They rose and went back to their poor
holdings, naked in the bleak light
of December. Their horizon contracted
to the one small, stone-filled field
with its tree, where the weather was nailing
the appalled body that had asked to be born.

R.S. THOMAS (1913–   )

Crucifixion.
Illuminated MS.

from: On the Morning of Christ's Nativity

This is the Month and this the happy morn
Wherein the Son of Heav'ns eternal King,
Of wedded Maid and Virgin Mother born,
Our great Redemption from above did bring;
For so the holy Sages once did sing,
   That he our deadly forfeit should release,
And with his Father work us a perpetual peace.

That glorious Form, that Light unsufferable,
And that far-beaming blaze of Majesty,
Wherewith he wont at Heav'ns high Councel-Table
To sit the midst of Trinal Unity,
He laid aside; and here with us to be,
   Forsook the Courts of everlasting Day,
And chose with us a darksom House of mortal Clay.

Say Heav'nly Muse, shall not thy sacred vein
Afford a Present to the Infant God?
Hast thou no verse, no hymn or solemn strein
To welcome him to this his new abode,
Now while the Heav'n by the Suns team untrod
   Hath took no print of the approaching light,
And all the spangled host keep watch in squadrons bright?

See how from far upon the Eastern rode
The Star-led Wizards haste with odours sweet,
O run, prevent them with thy humble ode,
And lay it lowly at his blessed feet;
Have thou the honour first, thy Lord to greet,
   And join thy voice unto the Angel Quire,
From out his secret Altar toucht with hallowed fire.

THE HYMN
It was the Winter wilde,
While the Heav'n-born-childe
   All meanly wrapt in the rude manger lies;
Nature in awe to him

Had doft her gaudy trim,
   With her great Master so to sympathize:
It was no season then for her
To wanton with the Sun her lusty Paramour.

Onely with speeches fair
She woo's the gentle Air
   To hide her guilty front with innocent Snow,
And on her naked shame,
Pollute with sinful blame,
   The Saintly Veil of Maiden white to throw,
Confounded that her Makers eyes
Should look so near upon her foul deformities.

But he her fears to cease
Sent down the meek-ey'd Peace,
   She crownd with Olive green, came softly sliding
Down through the turning sphear
His ready Harbinger,
   With Turtle wing the amorous clouds dividing,
And waving wide her mirtle wand
She strikes a universal Peace through Sea and Land.

No War, or Battels sound
Was heard the World around,
   The idle Spear and Shield were high up hung,
The hooked Chariot stood
Unstained with hostile blood,
   The Trumpet spake not to the armed throng,
And Kings sate still with awful eye,
As if they surely knew their sovran Lord was by.

But peaceful was the night
Wherein the Prince of light
   His reign of peace upon the earth began:
The Windes with wonder whist
Smoothly the waters kist,
   Whispering new joyes to the milde Ocean,
Who now hath quite forgot to rave,
While Birds of Calm sit brooding on the charmed wave.

JOHN MILTON (1608–1674)

The Nativity of Our Lord and Saviour Jesus Christ

Where is this stupendous stranger,
   Swains of Solyma, advise,
Lead me to my Master's manger,
   Shew me where my Saviour lies?

O Most Mighty! O Most Holy!
   Far beyond the seraph's thought,
Art thou then so mean and lowly
   As unheeded prophets taught?

O the magnitude of meekness!
   Worth from worth immortal sprung;
O the strength of infant weakness,
   If eternal is so young!

If so young and thus eternal,
   Michael tune the shepherd's reed,
Where the scenes are ever vernal,
   And the loves be love indeed!

See the God blasphem'd and doubted
   In the schools of Greece and Rome;
See the pow'rs of darkness routed,
   Taken at their utmost gloom.

Nature's decorations glisten
   Far above their usual trim;
Birds on box and laurel listen,
   As so near the cherubs hymn.

Boreas now no longer winters
   On the desolated coast;
Oaks no more are riv'n in splinters
   By the whirlwind and his host.

Spinks and ouzles sing sublimely,
 'We too have a Saviour born,'
Whiter blossoms burst untimely
 On the blest Mosaic thorn.

God all-bounteous, all-creative,
 Whom no ills from good dissuade,
Is incarnate, and a native
 Of the very world he made.

CHRISTOPHER SMART (1722–1771)

Virgin and Child. *Medieval stained glass*

At the Manger Mary Sings

O shut your bright eyes that mine must endanger
With their watchfulness; protected by its shade
Escape from my care: what can you discover
From my tender look but how to be afraid?
Love can but confirm the more it would deny.
    Close your bright eye.

Sleep. What have you learned from the womb that bore you
But an anxiety your Father cannot feel?
Sleep. What will the flesh that I gave do for you,
Or my mother love, but tempt you from His will?
Why was I chosen to teach His Son to weep?
    Little One, sleep.

Dream. In human dreams earth ascends to Heaven
Where no one need pray nor ever feel alone.
In your first few hours of life here, O have you
Chosen already what death must be your own?
How soon will you start on the Sorrowful Way?
    Dream while you may.

W.H. AUDEN (1907–74)

The Coronation of the Virgin. *Illuminated MS.*

Angel of the Annunciation. *Fra Angelico*

Sonnet

At the round earth's imagin'd corners, blow
Your trumpets, Angels, and arise, arise
From death, you numberless infinities
Of souls, and to your scatter'd bodies go,
All whom the flood did, and fire shall o'erthrow,
All whom war, dearth, age, agues, tyrannies,
Despair, law, chance, hath slain, and you whose eyes,
Shall behold God, and never taste death's woe.
But let them sleep, Lord, and me mourn a space,
For, if above all these, my sins abound,
'Tis late to ask abundance of Thy grace,
When we are there; here on this lowly ground,
Teach me how to repent; for that's as good
As if Thou hadst seal'd my pardon, with Thy blood.

JOHN DONNE (1573–1631)

Journey of the Magi

'A cold coming we had of it,
Just the worst time of the year
For a journey, and such a long journey:
The ways deep and the weather sharp,
The very dead of winter.'
And the camels galled, sore-footed, refractory,
Lying down in the melting snow
There were times we regretted
The summer palaces on slopes, the terraces,
And the silken girls bringing sherbet.
Then the camel men cursing and grumbling
And running away, and wanting their liquor and women,
And the night-fires going out, and the lack of shelters,
And the cities hostile and the towns unfriendly
And the villages dirty and charging high prices:
A hard time we had of it.
At the end we preferred to travel all night,
Sleeping in snatches.
With the voices singing in our ears, saying
That this was all folly.

Then at dawn we came down to a temperate valley,
Wet, below the snow line, smelling of vegetation:
With a running stream and a water-mill beating the darkness,
And three trees on the low sky,
And an old white horse galloped away in the meadow.
Then we came to a tavern with vine-leaves over the lintel,
Six hands at an open door dicing for pieces of silver,
And feet kicking the empty wine-skins.
But there was no information, and so we continued
And arrived at evening, not a moment too soon
Finding the place; it was (you may say) satisfactory.

All this was a long time ago, I remember.
And I would do it again, but set down
This set down
This: were we led all that way for

Birth or Death? There was a Birth, certainly,
We had evidence and no doubt. I had seen birth and death,
But had thought they were different; this Birth was
Hard and bitter agony for us, like Death, our death.
We returned to our places, these Kingdoms,
But no longer at ease here, in the old dispensation,
With an alien people clutching their gods.
I should be glad of another death.

T.S. ELIOT (1888–1965)

Adoration of the Magi. *Benedetto Bonfigli*

Prayer

Prayer the Churches banquet, Angels age,
    Gods breath in man returning to his birth,
    The soul in paraphrase, heart in pilgrimage,
The Christian plummet sounding heav'n and earth;
Engine against th' Almightie, sinners towre,
    Reversed thunder, Christ-side-piercing spear,
    The six-daies world transposing in an houre,
A kinde of tune, which all things heare and fear;
Softnesse, and peace, and joy, and love, and blisse,
    Exalted Manna, gladnesse of the best,
    Heaven in ordinarie, man well drest,
The milkie way, the bird of Paradise,
    Church-bels beyond the starres heard, the souls bloud,
    The land of spices; something understood.

GEORGE HERBERT (1593–1633)

Redemption

Having been tenant long to a rich Lord,
    Not thriving, I resolved to be bold,
    And make a suit unto him, to afford
A new small-rented lease, and cancell th' old.
In heaven at his manour I him sought:
    They told me there, that he was lately gone
    About some land, which he had dearly bought
Long since on earth, to take possession.
I straight return'd, and knowing his great birth,
    Sought him accordingly in great resorts;
    In cities, theatres, gardens, parks, and courts:
At length I heard a ragged noise and mirth
    Of thieves and murderers: there I him espied,
    Who straight, *Your suit is granted*, said, & died.

GEORGE HERBERT (1593–1633)

The Holy Innocents

Listen, the hay-bells tinkle as the cart
Wavers on rubber tires along the tar
And cindered ice below the burlap mill
And ale-wife run. The oxen drool and start
In wonder at the fenders of a car,
And blunder hugely up St Peter's hill.
These are the undefiled by women – their
Sorrow is not the sorrow of this world:
King Herod shrieking vengeance at the curled
Up knees of Jesus choking in the air,

A king of speechless clods and infants. Still
The world out-Herods Herod; and the year,
The nineteen-hundred forty-fifth of grace,
Lumbers with losses up the clinkered hill
Of our purgation; and the oxen near
The worn foundations of their resting-place,
The holy manger where their bed is corn
And holly torn for Christmas. If they die,
As Jesus, in the harness, who will mourn?
Lamb of the shepherds, Child, how still you lie.

ROBERT LOWELL (1917–1977)

Christ appearing to St Thomas, *Illuminated MS.*

On the Wounds of Our Crucified Lord

O these wakeful wounds of thine!
   Are they mouths? Or are they eyes?
Be they mouths or be they eyne,
   Each bleeding part some one supplies.

Lo, a mouth, whose full-bloom'd lips
   At too dear a rate are roses.
Lo, a bloodshot eye that weeps
   And many a cruel tear discloses.

O thou, that on this foot hast laid
   Many a kiss and many a tear,
Now thou shalt have all repaid
   Whatsoe'er thy charges were.

This foot hath got a mouth and lips
   To pay the sweet sum of thy kisses;
To pay thy tears, an eye that weeps
   Instead of tears such gems as this is.

The difference only this appears
   (Nor can the change offend),
The debt is paid in ruby tears
   Which thou in pearls did'st lend.

RICHARD CRASHAW (1613?–1649)

Mercy

From: *The Merchant of Venice*

The quality of mercy is not strained;
It droppeth as the gentle rain from heaven
Upon the place beneath. It is twice blest;
It blesseth him that gives and him that takes.
'Tis mightiest in the mightiest; it becomes
The thronèd monarch better than his crown.
His scepter shows the force of temporal power,
The attribute to awe and majesty,
Wherein doth sit the dread and fear of kings;
But mercy is above this scept'red sway;
It is enthronèd in the hearts of kings,
It is an attribute to God himself,
And earthly power doth then show likest God's
When mercy seasons justice.

WILLIAM SHAKESPEARE (1564–1616)

God's Grandeur

The world is charged with the grandeur of God.
   It will flame out, like shining from shook foil;
   It gathers to a greatness, like the ooze of oil
Crushed. Why do men then now not reck his rod?
Generations have trod, have trod, have trod;
   And all is seared with trade; bleared, smeared with toil;
   And wears man's smudge and shares man's smell: the soil
Is bare now, nor can foot feel, being shod.

And for all this, nature is never spent;
   Their lives the dearest freshness deep down things;
And though the last lights off the black West went
   Oh, morning, at the brown brink-eastward, springs –
Because the Holy Ghost over the bent
   World broods with warm breast and with ah! bright wings.

GERARD MANLEY HOPKINS (1844–1889)

Tintern Abbey

*Lines composed a few miles above Tintern Abbey, on
revisiting the banks of the Wye during a Tour.   July
13, 1798.*

Five years have past; five summers, with the length
Of five long winters! and again I hear
These waters, rolling from their mountain-springs
With a soft inland murmur. – Once again
Do I behold these steep and lofty cliffs,
That on a wild secluded scene impress
Thoughts of more deep seclusion; and connect
The landscape with the quiet of the sky.
The day is come when I again repose
Here, under this dark sycamore, and view
These plots of cottage-ground, these orchard-tufts,
Which at this season, with their unripe fruits,
Are clad in one green hue, and lose themselves
'Mid groves and copses. Once again I see
These hedge-rows, hardly hedge-rows, little lines
Of sportive wood run wild: these pastoral farms,
Green to the very door: and wreaths of smoke
Sent up, in silence, from among the trees!
With some uncertain notice, as might seem
Of vagrant dwellers in the houseless woods,
Or of some Hermit's cave, where by his fire
The Hermit sits alone.

        These beauteous forms
Through a long absence, have not been to me
As is a landscape to a blind man's eye:
But oft, in lonely rooms, and 'mid the din
Of towns and cities, I have owed to them,
In hours of weariness, sensations sweet,
Felt in the blood, and felt along the heart;
And passing even into my purer mind,
With tranquil restoration: – feelings too
Of unremembered pleasure: such, perhaps,
As have no slight or trivial influence

Tintern Abbey. *J.M.W. Turner*

On that best portion of a good man's life,
His little, nameless, unremembered, acts
Of kindness and of love. Nor less, I trust,
To them I may have owed another gift,
Of aspect more sublime; that blessed mood,
In which the burthen of the mystery,
In which the heavy and the weary weight
Of all this unintelligible world,
Is lightened: – that serene and blessed mood,
In which the affections gently lead us on, –
Until, the breath of this corporeal frame
And even the motion of our human blood
Almost suspended, we are laid asleep

In body, and become a living soul:
While with an eye made quiet by the power
Of harmony, and the deep power of joy,
We see into the life of things.

WILLIAM WORDSWORTH (1770–1850)

I Am the Great Sun
From a Normandy crucifix of 1632

I am the great sun, but you do not see me,
  I am your husband, but you turn away.
I am the captive, but you do not free me,
  I am the captain you will not obey.

I am the truth, but you will not believe me,
  I am the city where you will not stay,
I am your wife, your child, but you will leave me,
  I am that God to whom you will not pray.

I am your counsel, but you do not hear me,
  I am the lover whom you will betray,
I am the victor, but you do not cheer me,
  I am the holy dove whom you will slay.

I am your life, but if you will not name me,
Seal up your soul with tears, and never blame me.

CHARLES CAUSLEY (1917–   )

The Burning Babe

As I in hoary winter's night stood shivering in the snow,
Surprised I was with sudden heat which made my heart to
   glow;
And lifting up a fearful eye to view what fire was near,
A pretty babe all burning bright did in the air appear;
Who, scorchèd with excessive heat, such floods of tears did
   shed
As though his floods should quench his flames which with his
   tears were fed.
'Alas,' quoth he, 'but newly born in fiery heats I fry,
Yet none approach to warm their hearts or feel my fire but I!
My faultless breast the furnace is, the fuel wounding thorns,
Love is the fire, and sighs the smoke, the ashes shame and
   scorns,
The fuel Justice layeth on, and Mercy blows the coals,
The metal in this furnace wrought are men's defilèd souls,
For which, as now on fire I am to work them to their good,
So will I melt into a bath to wash them in my blood.'
With this he vanished out of sight and swiftly shrunk away,
And straight I callèd unto mind that it was Christmas day.

ROBERT SOUTHWELL (c.1561–1595)

from: Early Spring

The woods with living airs
   How softly fann'd,
Light airs from where the deep,
All down the sand,
Is breathing in his sleep,
   Heard by the land.

O follow, leaping blood,
   The season's lure!
O heart, look down and up
   Serene, secure,
Warm as the crocus cup,
   Like snowdrops, pure!

Past, Future glimpse and fade
   Thro' some slight spell,
A gleam from yonder vale,
   Some far blue fell,
And sympathies, how frail,
   In sound and smell!

Till at thy chuckled note,
   Thou twinkling bird,
The fairy fancies range,
   And, lightly stirr'd,
Ring little bells of change
   From word to word.

For now the Heavenly Power
   Makes all things new,
And thaws the cold, and fills
   The flower with dew;
The blackbirds have their wills,
   The poets too.

ALFRED, LORD TENNYSON (1809–1892)

Dover Beach

The sea is calm to-night,
The tide is full, the moon lies fair
Upon the Straits; – on the French coast, the light
Gleams, and is gone; the cliffs of England stand,
Glimmering and vast, out in the tranquil bay.
Come to the window, sweet is the night air!
Only, from the long line of spray
Where the sea meets the moon-blanch'd sand,
Listen! you hear the grating roar
Of pebbles which the waves suck back, and fling,
At their return, up the high strand,
Begin, and cease, and then again begin,
With tremulous cadence slow, and bring
The eternal note of sadness in.

Sophocles long ago
Heard it on the Aegaean, and it brought
Into his mind the turbid ebb and flow
Of human misery; we
Find also in the sound a thought,
Hearing it by this distant northern sea.

The sea of faith
Was once, too, at the full, and round earth's shore
Lay like the folds of a bright girdle furl'd;
But now I only hear
Its melancholy, long, withdrawing roar,
Retreating to the breath
Of the night-wind down the vast edges drear
And naked shingles of the world.

Ah, love, let us be true
To one another! for the world, which seems
To lie before us like a land of dreams,
So various, so beautiful, so new,
Hath really neither joy, nor love, nor light,

Nor certitude, nor peace, nor help for pain;
And we are here as on a darkling plain
Swept with confused alarms of struggle and flight,
Where ignorant armies clash by night.

MATTHEW ARNOLD (1822–1888)

Carrion Comfort

No worst, there is none. Pitched past pitch of grief,
More pangs will, schooled at forepangs, wilder wring.
Comforter, where, where is your comforting?
Mary, mother of us, where is your relief?
My cries heave, herds-long; huddle in a main, a chief
Woe, wórld-sorrow; on an áge-old anvil wince and sing –
Then lull, then leave off. Fury had shrieked 'No ling-
ering! Let me be fell: force I must be brief'.

  O the mind, mind has mountains; cliffs of fall
Frightful, sheer, no-man-fathomed. Hold them cheap
May who ne'er hung there. Nor does long our small
Durance deal with that steep or deep. Here! creep,
Wretch, under a comfort serves in a whirlwind: all
Life death does end and each day dies with sleep.

GERARD MANLEY HOPKINS (1844–1889)

Christ in the Grave. *Hans Holbein*

Written in Northampton County Asylum

I am! yet what I am who cares, or knows?
  My friends forsake me like a memory lost.
I am the self-consumer of my woes;
  They rise and vanish, an oblivious host,
Shadows of life, whose very soul is lost.
And yet I am – I live – though I am tossed

Into the nothingness of scorn and noise,
  Into the living sea of waking dream,
Where there is neither sense of life, nor joys,
  But the huge shipwreck of my own esteem
And all that's dear. Even those I loved the best
Are strange – nay, they are stranger than the rest.

I long for scenes where man has never trod –
  For scenes where woman never smiled or wept –
There to abide with my Creator, God,
  And sleep as I in childhood sweetly slept,
Full of high thoughts, unborn. So let me lie, –
The grass below; above, the vaulted sky.

JOHN CLARE (1793–1864)

The Lamb. *William Blake*

'La Sainte Face'. *Georges Rouault*

The Incarnate One

The windless northern surge, the sea-gull's scream,
And Calvin's kirk crowning the barren brae.
I think of Giotto the Tuscan shepherd's dream,
Christ, man and creature in their inner day.
How could our race betray
The Image, and the Incarnate One unmake
Who chose this form and fashion for our sake?

The Word made flesh here is made word again,
A word made word in flourish and arrogant crook.
See there King Calvin with his iron pen,
And God three angry letters in a book,
And there the logical hook
On which the Mystery is impaled and bent
Into an ideological instrument.

There's better gospel in man's natural tongue,
And truer sight was theirs outside the Law
Who saw the far side of the Cross among
The archaic peoples in their ancient awe,
In ignorant wonder saw
The wooden cross-tree on the bare hillside,
Not knowing that there a God suffered and died.

The fleshless word, growing, will bring us down,
Pagan and Christian man alike will fall,
The auguries say, the white and black and brown,
The merry and sad, theorist, lover, all
Invisibly will fall:
Abstract calamity, save for those who can
Build their cold empire on the abstract man.

A soft breeze stirs and all my thoughts are blown
Far out to sea and lost. Yet I know well
The bloodless word will battle for its own
Invisibly in brain and nerve and cell.
The generations tell
Their personal tale: the One has far to go
Past the mirages and the murdering snow.

EDWIN MUIR (1887–1959)

Justus quidem tu es, Domine, si, disputem tecum;
verumtamen justa loquar ad te: Quare via impiorum
prosperatur? &c.

Thou art indeed just, Lord, if I contend
With thee; but, sir, so what I plead is just.
Why do sinners' ways prosper? and why must
Disappointment all I endeavour end?
   Wert thou my enemy, O thou my friend,
How wouldst thou worse, I wonder, than thou dost
Defeat, thwart me? Oh, the sots and thralls of lust
Do in spare hours more thrive than I that spend,
Sir, life upon thy cause. See, banks and brakes
Now, leaved how thick! laced they are again
With fretty chervil, look, and fresh wind shakes
Them; birds build – but not I build; no, but strain,
Time's eunuch, and not breed one work that wakes.
Mine, O thou lord of life, send my roots rain.

GERARD MANLEY HOPKINS (1844–1849)

A song to John, Christ's Friend

Prey for us the Prince of Pees,
Amice Christi, Johannes.

To thee now, Christes dere derling,
That were a maiden bothe eld and ying,
Mine herte is set to thee to sing,
Amice Christi, Johannes.

For thou were so clene a may
The prevites of Hevene forsothe thou say
Whan on Christes brest thou lay,
Amice Christi, Johannes.

Whan Christ beforn Pilat was brought
Thou, clene maiden, forsok him nought:
To deye with him was all thy thought,
Amice Christi, Johannes.

Christes moder was thee betake,
A maiden to ben a maidenes make:
Thou be oure helpe we be not forsake,
Amice Christi, Johannes.

ANONYMOUS

Christ crowned with Thorns. *Albrecht Bouts*

from: The Dream of the Rood

So I lay there watching the Saviour's tree
Grieving in spirit for a long, long while,
Until I heard it utter sounds, the best
Of woods began to speak these words to me:
'It was long past – I still remember it –
That I was cut down at the copse's end,
Moved from my roots. Strong enemies there took me,
Told me to hold aloft their criminals,
Made me a spectacle. Men carried me
Upon their shoulders, set me on a hill,
A host of enemies there fastened me.
And then I saw the Lord of all mankind
Hasten with eager zeal that He might mount
Upon me. I durst not against God's word
Bend down or break, when I saw tremble all
The surface of the earth. Although I might
Have struck down all the foes, yet stood I fast.
Then the young hero (who was God Almighty)
Got ready, resolute and strong in heart.
He climbed onto the lofty gallows-tree,
Bold in the sight of many watching men,
When He intended to redeem mankind.

Translated by RICHARD HAMER

Sweet Death

The sweetest blossoms die.
   And so it was that, going day by day
   Unto the Church to praise and pray,
And crossing the green churchyard thoughtfully,
   I saw how on the graves the flowers
   Shed their fresh leaves in showers,
And how their perfume rose up to the sky
   Before it passed away.

The youngest blossoms die.
   They die and fall and nourish the rich earth
   From which they lately had their birth;
Sweet life, but sweeter death that passeth by
   And is as though it had not been: –
   All colours turn to green;
The bright hues vanish and the odours fly,
   The grass hath lasting worth.

And youth and beauty die.
   So be it, O my God, Thou God of truth:
   Better than beauty and than youth
Are Saints and Angels, a glad company;
   And Thou, O Lord, our Rest and Ease,
   Art better far than these.
Why should we shrink from our full harvest? why
   Prefer to glean with Ruth?

CHRISTINA ROSSETTI (1830–1894)

A Better Resurrection

I have no wit, no words, no tears;
    My heart within me like a stone
Is numbed too much for hopes or fears;
    Look right, look left, I dwell alone;
I lift mine eyes, but dimmed with grief
    No everlasting hills I see;
My life is in the falling leaf:
        O Jesus, quicken me.

My life is like a faded leaf,
    My harvest dwindled to a husk;
Truly my life is void and brief
    And tedious in the barren dusk;
My life is like a frozen thing,
    No bud nor greenness can I see:
Yet rise it shall – the sap of Spring;
        O Jesus, rise in me.

My life is like a broken bowl,
    A broken bowl that cannot hold
One drop of water for my soul
    Or cordial in the searching cold;
Cast in the fire the perished thing,
    Melt and remould it, till it be
A royal cup for Him my King:
        O Jesus, drink of me.

CHRISTINA ROSSETTI (1830–1894)

The Dying Christian to his Soul

Vital spark of heavenly flame!
Quit, O quit this mortal frame:
Trembling, hoping, ling'ring, flying,
O the pain, the bliss of dying!
Cease, fond Nature, cease thy strife,
And let me languish into life.

Hark! they whisper; angels say,
Sister Spirit, come away!
What is this absorbs me quite!
Steals my senses, shuts my sight,
Drowns my spirits, draws my breath?
Tell me, my soul, can this be death?

The world recedes; it disappears!
Heaven opens on my eyes! my ears
With sounds seraphic ring!
Lend, lend your wings! I mount! I fly!
O Grave! where is thy victory?
O Death! where is thy sting?

ALEXANDER POPE (1688–1744)

Sunday Morning, King's, Cambridge

File into yellow candle light, fair choristers of King's
   Lost in the shadowy silence of canopied Renaissance stalls
In blazing glass above the dark glow skies and thrones and
     wings
   Blue, ruby, gold and green between the whiteness of the walls
And with what rich precision the stonework soars and springs
   To fountain out a spreading vault – a shower that never falls.

The white of windy Cambridge courts, the cobbles brown and
     dry,
   The gold of plaster Gothic with ivy overgrown,
The apple-red, the silver fronts, the wide green flats and high,
   The yellowing elm-trees circled out on islands of their own –
Oh, here behold all colours change that catch the flying sky
   To waves of pearly light that heave along the shafted stone.

In far East Anglian churches, the clasped hands lying long
   Recumbent on sepulchral slabs or effigied in brass
Buttress with prayer this vaulted roof so white and light and
     strong
   And countless congregations as the generations pass
Join choir and great crowned organ case, in centuries of song
   To praise Eternity contained in Time and coloured glass.

JOHN BETJEMAN (1906–   )

from: The Prologue to The Canterbury Tales

The Parson

A good man was ther of religioun,
And was a povre Persoun of a toun;
But riche he was of holy thoght and werk.
He was also a lerned man, a clerk,
That Cristes gospel trewely wolde preche;
His parisshens devoutly wolde he teche.
Benigne he was, and wonder diligent,
And in adversitee ful pacient;
And switch he was y-preved ofte sythes.
Ful looth were him to cursen for his tythes,
But rather wolde he yeven, out of doute,
Un-to his povre parisshens aboute
Of his offring, and eek of his substaunce.
He coude in litel thing han suffisaunce.
Wyd was his parisshe, and houses fer a-sonder,
But he ne lafte nat, for reyn ne thonder,
In siknes nor in meschief, to visyte
The ferreste in his parisshe, much and lyte,
To drawen folk to heven by fairnesse
By good ensample, was his bisinesse:
But it were any personne obstinat,
What-so he were, of heigh or lowe estat,
Him wolde he snibben sharply for the nones.
A bettre preest, I trowe that nowher noon is.
He wayted after no pompe and reverence,
Ne maked him a spyced conscience,
But Cristes lore, and his apostles twelve,
He taughte, and first he folwed it himselve.

GEOFFREY CHAUCER (?1340–1400)

The Creation. *Illuminated MS.*

The Usk

Christ is the language which we speak to God
And also God, so that we speak in truth;
He in us, we in him, speaking
To one another, to him, the City of God.

I. Such a fool as I am you had better ignore
   Tongue twist, malevolent, fat mouthed
   I have no language but that other one
   His the Devil's, no mouse I, creeping out of the cheese
   With a peaked cap scanning the distance
   Looking for truth.
   Words when I have them, come out, the Devil
   Encouraging, grinning from the other side of the street
   And my tears
   Streaming, a blubbered face, when I am not laughing
   Where in all this
   Is calm, measure,
   Exactness
   The Lord's peace?

II. Nothing is in my own voice because I have not
    Any. Nothing in my own name
    Here inscribed on water, nothing but flow
    A ripple, outwards. Standing beside the Usk
    You flow like truth, river, I will get in
    Over me, through me perhaps, river let me be crystalline
    As I shall not be, shivering upon the bank.
    A swan passed. So is it, the surface, sometimes
    Benign like a mirror, but not I passing, the bird.

III. Under the bridge, meet reward, the water
     Falling in cascades or worse, you devil, for truthfulness
     Is no part of the illusion, the clear sky
     Is not yours, the water
     Falling not yours
     Only the sheep
     Munching at the river brim
     Perhaps

IV. What I had hoped for, the clear line
Tremulous like water but
Clear also to the stones underneath
Has not come that way, for my truth
Was not public enough, nor perhaps true.
Holy Father, Almighty God
Stop me before I speak

             – *per Christum.*

V. Lies on my tongue. Get up and bolt the door
For I am coming not to be believed
The messenger of anything I say.
So I am come, stand in the cold tonight
The servant of the grain upon my tongue,
Beware, I am the man, and let me in.

VI. So speech is treasured, for the things it gives
Which I can not have, for I speak too plain
Yet not so plain as to be understood
It is confusion and a madman's tongue.
Where drops the reason, there is no one by.
Torture my mind: and so swim through the night
As envy cannot touch you, or myself
Sleep comes, and let her, warm at my side, like death.
The Holy Spirit and the Holy One
Of Israel be my guide. So among tombs
Truth may be sought, and found, if we rejoice
With Ham and Shem and Japhet in the dark
The ark rolls onward over a wide sea.
Come sleep, come lightning, comes the dove at last.

             C. H. SISSON (1914–   )

Our Lady of Walsingham

There once the penitents took off their shoes
And then walked barefoot the remaining mile;
And the small trees, a stream and hedgerows file
Slowly along the munching English lane,
Like cows to the old shrine, until you lose
Track of your dragging pain.

The stream flows down under the druid tree,
Shiloah's whirlpools gurgle and make glad
The castle of God. Sailor, you were glad
And whistled Sion by that stream. But see:

Our Lady, too small for her canopy,
Sits near the altar. There's no comeliness
At all or charm in that expressionless
Face with its heavy eyelids. As before,
This face, for centuries a memory,
Non est species, neque decor,
Expressionless, expresses God: it goes
Past castled Sion. She knows what God knows,
Not Calvary's Cross nor crib at Bethlehem
Now, and the world shall come to Walsingham.

ROBERT LOWELL (1917–1977)

Blisful Ordre of Wedlok

From: The Merchant's Tale

A wyf! a! Siente Marie, *ben'cite!*
How mighte a man han any adversitee
That hath a wyf? certes, I can nat seye.
The blisse which that is bitwixe hem tweye
Ther may no tonge telle, or herte thinke.
If he be povre, she helpeth him to swinke;
She kepeth his good, and wasteth never a deel;
Al that hir housebonde lust, hir lyketh weel;
She seith not ones 'nay,' when he seith 'ye.'
'Do this,' seith he; 'al redy, sir,' seith she.
O blisful ordre of wedlok precious,
Thou art so mery, and eek so vertuous,
And so commended and appreved eek,
That every man that halt him worth a leek,
Up-on his bare knees oghte al his lyf
Thanken his god that him hath sent a wyf;
Or elles preye to god him for to sende
A wyf, to laste un-to his lyves ende.

GEOFFREY CHAUCER (?1340–1400)

Frescoes in an Old Church

Six centuries now have gone
Since, one by one,
These stones were laid,
And in air's vacancy
This beauty made.

They who thus reared them
Their long rest have won;
Ours now this heritage –
To guard, preserve, delight in, brood upon;
And in these transitory fragments scan
The immortal longings in the soul of Man.

WALTER DE LA MARE (1873–1956)

Holy Thursday

'Twas on a Holy Thursday, their innocent faces clean,
The children walking two and two, in red and blue and green,
Grey-headed beadles walked before, with wands as white as
 snow,
Till into the high dome of Paul's they like Thames' waters flow.
O what a multitude they seemed, these flowers of London
 town!
Seated in companies they sit with radiance all their own.
The hum of multitudes was there, but multitudes of lambs,
Thousands of little boys and girls raising their innocent hands.
Now like a mighty wind they raise to Heaven the voice of song,
Or like harmonious thunderings the seats of Heaven among.
Beneath them sit the agèd men, wise guardians of the poor;
Then cherish pity, lest you drive an angel from your door.

WILLIAM BLAKE (1757–1827)

St Christopher: Breage, Cornwall

Egocentric

What care I if God be
If he be not good to me,
If he will not hear my cry
Nor heed my melancholy midnight sigh?
What care I if he created Lamb,
And golden Lion, and mud-delighting Clam,
And Tiger stepping out on padded toe,
And the fecund earth the Blindworms know?

He made the Sun, the Moon and every Star,
He made the infant Owl and the Baboon,
He made the ruby-orbed Pelican,
He made all silent inhumanity,
Nescient and quiescent to his will,
Unquickened by the questing conscious flame
That is my glory and my bitter bane.
What care I if Skies are blue,
If God created Gnat and Gnu,
What care I if good God be
If he be not good to me?

STEVIE SMITH (1903–1971)

The Sheep of His Pasture. *Edward Calvert*

from: *Elegy Written in a Country Churchyard*

The curfew tolls the knell of parting day,
   The lowing herd wind slowly o'er the lea,
The plowman homeward plods his weary way,
   And leaves the world to darkness and to me.

Now fades the glimmering landscape on the sight,
   And all the air a solemn stillness holds,
Save where the beetle wheels his droning flight,
   And drowsy tinklings lull the distant folds;

Save that from yonder ivy-mantled tower
   The moping owl does to the moon complain
Of such as, wand'ring near her secret bower,
   Molest her ancient solitary reign.

Coming from Evening Church. *Samuel Palmer*

Beneath those rugged elms, that yew-tree's shade,
    Where heaves the turf in many a mould'ring heap,
Each in his narrow cell for ever laid,
    The rude forefathers of the hamlet sleep.

The breezy call of incense-breathing morn,
    The swallow twitt'ring from the straw-built shed,
The cock's shrill clarion, or the echoing horn,
    No more shall rouse them from their lowly bed.

For them no more the blazing hearth shall burn,
    Or busy housewife ply her evening care:
No children run to lisp their sire's return,
    Or climb his knees the envied kiss to share.

Oft did the harvest to their sickle yield,
    Their furrow oft the stubborn glebe has broke:
How jocund did they drive their team afield!
    How bowed the woods beneath their sturdy stroke!

Let not Ambition mock their useful toil,
    Their homely joys, and destiny obscure;
Nor Grandeur hear with a disdainful smile
    The short and simple annals of the poor.

The boast of heraldry, the pomp of power,
    And all that beauty, all that wealth e'er gave,
Awaits alike th' inevitable hour:
    The paths of glory lead but to the grave.

Nor you, ye proud, impute to These the fault,
    If Memory o'er their tomb no trophies raise,
Where through the long-drawn aisle and fretted vault
    The pealing anthem swells the note of praise.

Can storied urn or animated bust
  Back to its mansion call the fleeting breath?
Can Honour's voice provoke the silent dust,
  Or Flatt'ry soothe the dull cold ear of death?

Perhaps in this neglected spot is laid
  Some heart once pregnant with celestial fire;
Hands, that the rod of empire might have swayed,
  Or waked to ecstasy the living lyre.

But Knowledge to their eyes her ample page
  Rich with the spoils of time did ne'er unroll;
Chill Penury repressed their noble rage,
  And froze the genial current of the soul.

THOMAS GRAY (1716–1771)

Stoke Poges Church

From: Henry V

King Henry
O God of battles, steel my soldiers' hearts;
Possess them not with fear; take from them now
The sense of reckoning, if th'opposèd numbers
Pluck their hearts from them. Not today, O Lord,
O not today, think not upon the fault
My father made in compassing the crown!
I Richard's body have interrèd new,
And on it have bestowed more contrite tears
Than from it issued forcèd drops of blood.
Five hundred poor I have in yearly pay,
Who twice a day their withered hands hold up
Toward heaven, to pardon blood: and I have built
Two chantries where the sad and solemn priests
Sing still for Richard's soul. More will I do,
Though all that I can do is nothing worth,
Since that my penitence comes after all,
Imploring pardon.

WILLIAM SHAKESPEARE (1564–1616)

Christ in Majesty. *Illuminated MS.*

The Universal Prayer

Father of all! in every age,
  In every clime adored,
By saint, by savage, and by sage,
  Jehovah, Jove, or Lord!

Thou great First Cause, least understood!
  Who all my sense confined
To know but this, that Thou art good,
  And that myself am blind;

Yet gave me in this dark estate,
  To see the good from ill:
And binding nature fast in fate,
  Left free the human will.

       * * *

To Thee, whose temple is all space,
  Whose altar, earth, sea, skies,
One chorus let all being raise;
  All nature's incense rise!

ALEXANDER POPE (1688–1744)

THE INFANT ST.JOHN.

The Infant St John. *Painted glass*

Acknowledgments

The editor and publishers would like to thank the following for permission to reproduce certain copyright poems:

W.H. Auden, *At the Manger* from COLLECTED POEMS. Reprinted by permission of Faber and Faber Ltd.

John Betjeman, *Sunday Morning, Kings, Cambridge* and *Holy Trinity, Sloane Street* from COLLECTED POEMS. Reprinted by permission of John Murray (Publishers) Ltd.

Charles Causley, *I am the Great Sun* from COLLECTED POEMS Reprinted by permission of Macmillan, London and Basingstoke.

T.S. Eliot, *Journey of the Magi* from COLLECTED POEMS 1909–1962. Reprinted by permission of Faber and Faber Ltd.

Richard Hamer, *The Dream of the Rood* from A CHOICE OF ANGLO SAXON VERSE by Richard Hamer. Reprinted by permission of Faber and Faber Ltd.

Robert Lowell, *The Holy Innocents* and *Our Lady of Walsingham* from POEMS 1938–1949. Reprinted by permission of Faber and Faber Ltd.

Walter de la Mare, *Frescoes in an Old Church*. Reprinted by permission of The Literary Trustees of Walter de la Mare and The Society of Authors as their representative.

Edwin Muir, *The Annunciation* and *The Incarnate One* from THE COLLECTED POEMS OF EDWIN MUIR. Reprinted by permission of Faber and Faber Ltd.

C.H. Sisson, *The Usk* from IN THE TROJAN DITCH. Reprinted by permission of Carcanet Press Ltd.

Stevie Smith, *God and the Devil* and *Egocentric* from THE COLLECTED POEMS OF STEVIE SMITH published by Allen Lane. Reprinted by permission of James MacGibbon.

R.S. Thomas, *Hill Christmas* from LABORATORIES OF THE SPIRIT by R.S. Thomas. Reprinted by permission of Macmillan, London and Basingstoke.

Index of Poets and Artists